HOW TO MAKE ICE CREAM

51 Recipes for Classic and Contemporary Flavors

Nicole Weston

Storey Publishing

The mission of Storey Publishing is to serve our customers by publishing practical information that encourages personal independence in harmony with the environment.

Edited by Margaret Sutherland and Mollie Firestone
Series design by Alethea Morrison
Art direction by Jeff Stiefel
Text production by Theresa Wiscovitch

Cover illustration by © Elena Bulay
Interior illustrations by © Holly Exley

Storey Publishing
210 MASS MoCA Way
North Adams, MA 01247
www.storey.com

Printed in the United States by McNaughton & Gunn, Inc.
10 9 8 7 6 5 4 3 2 1

LIBRARY OF CONGRESS CATALOGING-IN-PUBLICATION DATA

Weston, Nicole, author.
  How to make ice cream : 51 recipes for classic and contemporary
  flavors / by Nicole Weston.
      pages cm. — (A storey basics)
  Includes index.
  ISBN 978-1-61212-388-2 (pbk. : alk. paper)
  ISBN 978-1-61212-389-9 (ebook) 1. Ice cream, ices, etc. I. Title.
TX795.W484 2015
641.8'62—dc23
                                    2014033767

CONTENTS

ICE CREAM RECIPES

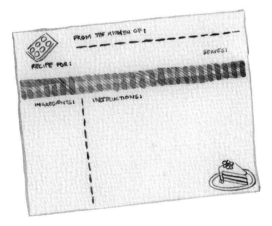

PART ONE

INTRODUCTION TO ICE CREAM

On a hot summer day, very few things taste as good as a bowl full of ice cream. Ice cream is a treat that appeals to people of all ages, from kids waiting in line for a cone at an ice cream truck after school to adults indulging in a scoop of some specialty flavor as a component of a plated dessert at a fine dining restaurant. It is unique because it is rich and indulgent, yet it often reminds us of our childhoods. It can serve as dessert in its own right, and it can accompany other desserts as a side. And because of its ubiquitousness in grocery store freezer cases, we sometimes forget just how special ice cream really is.

Homemade ice cream is even more special than anything that an ice cream truck, a restaurant, or a grocery store can deliver. You can not only customize the flavors and ingredients to create your favorite flavors, but you'll probably also be surprised by just how easy it is to make it yourself. Homemade ice cream can rival premium store-bought ice creams and can easily eclipse the less expensive brands with superior flavors and a richer texture. The only downside to starting to make your own ice creams at home is that you may find it difficult to go back to store-bought — unless you're simply searching the grocery store aisle for inspiration for your own flavor creations.

WHAT IS ICE CREAM?

AT ITS MOST BASIC, ice cream is a mixture of frozen cream and a sweetener, paired with a flavoring agent of some kind, such as vanilla, fruit, or chocolate. There are two main styles of ice cream. **French-style ice cream** starts with a cooked custard base made with milk, cream, sugar, and either eggs or egg yolks. This ice cream base is very thick, with an almost puddinglike consistency before it is churned. It produces a very rich ice cream with a velvety smooth texture and a slightly eggy flavor. **American-style ice cream,** also known as Philadelphia-style ice cream, typically has a lighter and more fluid consistency than that of French-style ice creams. It is made with milk, cream, sugar, and flavorings, but it does not contain eggs. It has a more pronounced dairy taste that is a good base for other flavors to be added.

Neither of these two styles of ice cream is better than the other. It all comes down to personal preference when you are making your recipes. Some people prefer the richer, eggier French-style ice cream, and others prefer the lighter and simpler taste of the American-style ice cream. And plenty of ice cream fans like both styles equally well. I like the consistency of both types of ice cream and find that some flavors work better with one base than the other. Fruit ice creams, for instance, have a brighter flavor when they are made with an American-style base because the added richness of the eggs in the French-style ice cream can mute the flavor of the fruit. Chocolate ice creams, however, can feel even more decadent and mousse-like on the tongue when made with a French-style base.

HOW ICE CREAM IS MADE

ICE CREAM IS NOT MADE BY simply pouring cream into a freezer. Ice cream is made by quickly freezing a flavored base mixture while agitating it, whether you are vigorously shaking it or slowly stirring it. Fast freezing allows the mixture to set up without forming large ice crystals that would result in a finished product that was more like a chunky snow cone than a silky smooth cream.

Agitating the ice cream base has two functions. First, the motion helps the base cool down very quickly and prevents large ice crystals from developing as it chills. Second, agitation adds air to the mixture as it freezes, which creates an ice cream with a soft texture that will be scoopable when frozen. That added air also makes ice cream taste better, because slight aeration allows the frozen mixture to melt smoothly and evenly on your tongue.

The first real ice cream recipes appeared in the early to mid eighteenth century. These recipes called for a small container of cream to be placed inside a larger container packed with ice and salt. The cream was churned or stirred in this insulated environment until it took on a more solid, scoopable consistency. The salt lowered the freezing temperature of the ice, creating a very cold environment where the cream could freeze quickly and smoothly. This process was generally done by hand and was labor-intensive, especially if the ice cream was going to be served to a large group. But like all great things, ice cream attracted innovation to make it easier to produce and more accessible. A patent for the first hand-cranked, home ice cream maker was issued in 1843 and was a huge step in streamlining the production process. An even bigger step was the propagation of refrigeration, which allowed ice cream to be prepared in bulk, shipped to more people, and stored for long periods of time.

Ingredients

As with most homemade recipes, if you start with the best quality ingredients that you can find, your finished product will have the best possible flavor. High-quality cream and milk will give your ice cream a rich dairy flavor that you will be able to taste in every bite. These recipes typically call for heavy cream or heavy whipping cream, and whole milk. The fat in these products is what makes ice cream both light and rich. There is no substitute for the heavy cream. Whole milk will definitely give you the best results, but you can substitute reduced-fat milk to make the ice cream a little bit lighter without giving up much of the texture of the original recipe.

The sugar in an ice cream base also plays an important role in the finished product. It not only sweetens the ice cream and allows other flavors to stand out, but it also contributes to the creamy, soft texture of ice cream by discouraging the formation of ice crystals in the base as it freezes. You can experiment with reducing the sugar in some recipes to suit your tastes, but keep in mind that the finished ice cream will always taste a little less sweet than the unfrozen ice cream base and that your ice cream may have a slightly icier texture than one made with the full amount of sugar.

Cooking the Ice Cream Base

Some of the ice cream recipes in this book have only a minimally cooked base, where milk is heated just to dissolve sugar, cocoa powder, or other ingredients. This base will have a consistency that is only slightly thickened, and it is always easy to make. Some of these ice creams have a custard base that includes tempered eggs and may take a little extra time to make.

Eggs are tempered when a hot liquid, such as milk, is carefully streamed into them, bringing the eggs up to a very high temperature without cooking them. When properly incorporated, eggs have thickening properties that will help bring a custard to the appropriate consistency. Eggs need to be tempered because they cook very quickly and can easily turn to scrambled eggs instead of custard if not treated gently.

TEMPERING EGGS hot milk

eggs

To temper eggs or egg yolks, you need a large bowl and a whisk. Give the eggs a brief whisk in the bowl to break them up. Take your hot milk mixture and, working with just a few teaspoons at a time, pour it into the eggs as you whisk continuously. Adding the milk this slowly prevents the eggs from being cooked instantly from exposure to heat. Keep adding the milk in very small increments until all of it has been added. When you return the mixture to the heat of the stove, the eggs will start to thicken the ice cream base.

It is easy to see that an ice cream base is thickening as it cooks, but it can be difficult to tell when it is done. In general, it only takes a couple of minutes for the base to thicken when it is cooking. It should be stirred constantly to prevent it from burning or sticking to the bottom of the pan. One easy way to check for thickness is to see if the mixture will coat the back of a spoon. This means that you can stick a spoon into your cooking custard, pull it out, and run your finger down the back of the spoon. If the mixture does not run and the little path you have drawn holds its shape, your custard is coating the back of a spoon and is finished cooking.

CHOOSING AN ICE CREAM MAKER

THESE DAYS, MAKING ICE CREAM IS a much less time-consuming process than it once was thanks to a wide selection of small, fast, home ice cream makers that allow you to churn a batch in about the same amount of time it takes to run to the store and pick up a container. Home ice cream makers will chill an ice cream base very quickly while adding air to it. Chilling it quickly reduces the number and size of ice crystals in the finished product, so the ice cream will be smooth and creamy when it is ready to eat. A wide variety of ice cream makers are on the market at a wide variety of price points. They also come in a wide variety of sizes, so with a little bit of comparison shopping you are sure to find something that will fit both your kitchen and needs.

There are three main types of ice cream makers. The most basic kind is a **hand-churn ice cream maker**. For this type of gadget, you need to add your own ice and salt to one chamber and your ice cream base to the other. Then you shake or crank the churn while the base thickens. These machines tend to be inexpensive and make softer ice creams, but they work and will give you a workout as you churn each batch.

The most common type is the **canister ice cream maker**. This model has a thick-walled canister that you freeze in advance, and you simply pour your base into the frozen canister and churn away. Canister ice cream makers are typically small, countertop appliances that are about the size of a food processor. You can also buy canister attachments to work with other appliances, like stand mixers, so you won't need a whole new appliance just to make ice cream. The downside to this type of appliance is that you need to do some advance planning, making sure to put the canister in the freezer about 24 hours before you want to make your ice cream, and you will not be able to use it on short notice. Like the hand churn ice cream maker, this type of machine can only churn one batch at a time.

**hand-churn
ice cream maker**

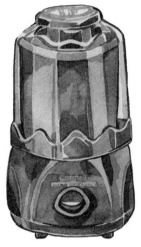

**canister
ice cream maker**

**compressor
ice cream maker**

The most expensive kind is a **compressor ice cream maker**. The internal compressor starts to freeze your base as soon as you turn it on, so you don't need to prefreeze anything, and you don't even need to chill your base before adding it to the machine, although that will speed up the freezing process. The advantage to this type of ice cream maker is that the machine is always ready to go and is capable of making multiple batches, one right after another, with no waiting time. This type of machine is not ideal for the occasional ice cream maker, but if you love to make ice cream or find that you are often serving a crowd, you can get a lot of use out of one of these.

CHURNING, STORING, AND SCOOPING HOMEMADE ICE CREAM

EVERY ICE CREAM MAKER IS going to have slightly different instructions, so it is important that you read the directions before using yours. Some automatically shut off after the ice cream gets thick enough. Others need to be manually shut off when the ice cream is thick and creamy. Homemade ice cream is generally done when it reaches the consistency of soft-serve ice cream, as it will not become rock solid in an ice cream maker. You will need to transfer your soft ice cream to a freezer-safe container and pop it into the freezer for a few hours for it to firm up to a scoopable consistency, though you can eat the soft-serve version straight out of the ice cream maker if you wish!

Any mix-ins that you want to incorporate into your ice cream should be added when it is soft and freshly churned. Nuts, chocolate chips, and fresh fruit should not be added while the ice cream maker is churning your ice cream base, because large chunks can prevent the machine from churning properly and can even cause the machine to become stuck. Caramel or fudge swirls, which you can easily add in by using store-bought ice cream sauces, should also be added after the ice cream is churned. If you add them during churning, they will be completely folded into the ice cream and you'll have a different flavor ice cream, rather than a swirl.

Ice cream should always be stored in an airtight container in the freezer to discourage ice crystals from forming. Depending on how cold your freezer is, most of these ice creams should be scoopable straight from the freezer. If your ice cream is too hard, run your scoop under hot water and then use it to form a scoop. Avoid softening the whole container of ice cream too much, as it could refreeze with ice crystals and lose some of its creamy consistency. Most store-bought ice creams don't have this problem (except after excessive softening) because they have added emulsifiers and stabilizers to maintain their texture over long periods of storage. Fortunately, homemade ice cream is made in small batches and tends to get eaten very quickly, so you will probably only have to worry about storing it for a week or so at a time! For long-term storage, airtight containers can keep the ice cream fresh for a few months in the freezer.

WORKING WITHOUT AN ICE CREAM MAKER

ICE CREAM MAKERS HELP you create ice cream quickly and easily, but it is possible to make ice cream without an ice cream maker. One method of doing this is by hand-stirring your ice cream. To do this, simply make the ice cream base of your choice and pour it into a large baking dish. Place the baking dish in the freezer, then come back and give the mixture a thorough stir with a fork after 15 to 20 minutes. This helps break up any large ice crystals that might be forming. Check back every 15 to 20 minutes, and repeat the stirring process until the ice cream becomes thick and is mostly frozen. The process can take as little as 1½ to 2 hours if you have a very shallow container and can freeze the ice cream base quickly, but can take longer if you are using a deeper bowl. When the ice cream is thick enough to scoop, you can stir in any mix-ins that the recipe might call for, and you can serve your ice cream or transfer it to an airtight container for longer storage.

Another method is to make a style of ice cream that does not require any churning at all. These no-churn ice creams are typically aerated with whipped cream, rather than the churning of an ice cream maker. They have a very different method for making them than most ice cream bases, and you can find an entire chapter of these recipes at the end of this book.

PART TWO

ICE CREAM RECIPES

Now that you have the basic knowledge of what ingredients and equipment you need to make ice cream at home, it is time to get into the recipes. The section covers the traditional ice cream recipes and includes both French-style ice creams and American-style ice creams, and you'll find recipes that range from timeless classics to more creative flavor combinations.

VANILLA, CHOCOLATE, AND COFFEE

American-Style Vanilla Bean

Vanilla ice cream should be a staple in everyone's freezer. It is delicious on its own and goes well with every dessert from chocolate chip cookies to homemade apple pie. This classic ice cream is an excellent choice for all occasions. It is an American-style ice cream, which means that it doesn't contain any eggs. You get a good fresh cream and clear vanilla flavor in every scoop of this ice cream. Using a whole vanilla bean adds great flavor and also gives it a nice finished look.

> 2 cups heavy cream
> 1½ cups whole milk
> ¾ cup sugar
> 1 vanilla bean

1. Combine cream, milk, and sugar in a medium saucepan. Split the vanilla bean lengthwise down the center and add it to the milk mixture. Bring to a simmer, stirring until the sugar is dissolved. Remove from heat. Cover and let cool to room temperature.

2. Remove the vanilla bean and scrape out the vanilla seeds using the back of a knife. Add the seeds to the milk mixture and discard the pod, or set aside for another use.

3. Cover and refrigerate until well chilled, 3 to 4 hours, or overnight.

4. Pour chilled mixture into an ice cream maker and freeze as directed.

5. Transfer ice cream to a freezer-safe container and place in the freezer. Allow it to firm up for 1 to 2 hours before serving.

Makes about 1 quart

French-Style Vanilla Bean

French vanilla is right up there with American-style vanilla ice cream as a favorite for ice cream lovers. This recipe is made with eggs, so the base has a thicker consistency than the plain vanilla does, and it has a texture that is a little richer, meaning it will coat the inside of your mouth with vanilla flavor. Because it includes eggs, you can taste a hint of egginess in the finished ice cream that adds to this flavor's rich character. Vanilla bean is a must-use ingredient for vanilla fans, as it will infuse the ice cream with the best vanilla flavor.

- 1½ cups heavy cream
- 1½ cups whole milk
- ⅔ cup sugar
- 1 vanilla bean
- 4 large egg yolks

1. Combine cream, milk, and sugar in a large saucepan. Split the vanilla bean lengthwise down the center and add it to the milk mixture. Bring to a simmer, stirring until the sugar is dissolved. Remove from heat. Cover and let cool to room temperature. Remove vanilla bean and set aside.

(continued on next page)

2. Bring milk mixture back up to a simmer.

3. Whisk together egg yolks in a large bowl. When the milk mixture comes to a simmer, remove from heat and very slowly stream it into the egg yolk mixture to temper it while whisking constantly. When all the milk mixture has been added, return it to the saucepan and continue to cook over medium heat, stirring constantly, until the mixture has thickened enough to coat the back of a spoon, 2 to 3 minutes. Remove from heat.

4. Scrape the vanilla seeds out of the pod you used to infuse the milk with the back of a knife. Add the seeds to the milk mixture and discard the pod, or set aside for another use.

5. Cover milk mixture and allow to cool to room temperature, then refrigerate until well chilled, 3 to 4 hours, or overnight.

6. Pour chilled mixture into an ice cream maker and freeze as directed.

7. Transfer ice cream to a freezer-safe container and place in the freezer. Allow it to firm up for 1 to 2 hours before serving.

Makes about 1 quart

Dark Chocolate

Many chocolate lovers favor dark chocolate over milk chocolate because it has a more intense cocoa flavor. In ice cream, you'll still get some dairy notes along with your dark chocolate, but chocoholics will get that deep flavor in this ice cream, which uses a combination of cocoa powder and melted dark chocolate to highlight the bittersweet flavor of dark chocolate.

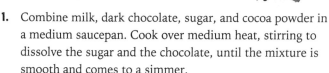

- 1 cup whole milk
- 4 ounces dark chocolate, chopped
- ⅔ cup sugar
- ¼ cup cocoa powder
- 3 large egg yolks
- 2 cups heavy cream
- 1 teaspoon vanilla extract

1. Combine milk, dark chocolate, sugar, and cocoa powder in a medium saucepan. Cook over medium heat, stirring to dissolve the sugar and the chocolate, until the mixture is smooth and comes to a simmer.

2. Whisk together egg yolks in a large bowl. When the milk mixture comes to a simmer, remove from heat and very slowly stream it into the egg yolk mixture to temper it while whisking constantly. When all the milk mixture has been added, return it to the saucepan and continue to cook over medium heat, stirring constantly, until the mixture has thickened enough to coat the back of a spoon, 2 to 3 minutes. Remove from heat and stir in cream and vanilla.

(continued on next page)

3. Cool to room temperature, then cover and refrigerate until well chilled, 3 to 4 hours, or overnight.

4. Pour chilled mixture into an ice cream maker and freeze as directed.

5. Transfer ice cream to a freezer-safe container and place in the freezer. Allow it to firm up for 1 to 2 hours before serving.

Makes about 1 quart

Chocolate Chip

Chocolate chip ice cream is one ice cream flavor that I never get tired of. It's vanilla — with chocolate! The trick with chocolate chip ice cream is making the chocolate chips. Chopped-up chocolate will become much too hard when it is in ice cream. It will be hard to chew and, since it won't have time to melt in your mouth, you won't be able to taste much of the chocolate flavor. Adding a little bit of vegetable oil to the melted chocolate gives it just the right consistency when frozen.

1½ cups whole milk

¾ cup sugar

2 cups heavy cream

2 teaspoons vanilla extract

3 ounces dark or semisweet chocolate, coarsely chopped

2 teaspoons vegetable oil

1. Combine milk and sugar in a medium saucepan. Bring to a simmer, stirring until the sugar is dissolved. Remove from heat and stir in heavy cream and vanilla.

2. Cover and refrigerate until well chilled, 3 to 4 hours, or overnight.

3. Pour chilled mixture into an ice cream maker and freeze as directed.

4. While ice cream is freezing, combine the chocolate and vegetable oil in a small microwave-safe bowl. Microwave on medium power in 30- to 40-second intervals, stirring regularly, until chocolate is melted and mixture is smooth.

5. When ice cream is churned, drizzle the chocolate mixture into the ice cream as you transfer it to a freezer-safe container, creating ribbons of chocolate that will break up as you stir it gently. Incorporate all of the chocolate mixture. Place ice cream in freezer and allow it to firm up for 1 to 2 hours before serving.

Makes about 1 quart

American-Style Chocolate

This is classic chocolate ice cream at its best. As an American-style ice cream, this recipe doesn't use any eggs, yet it still has a silky smooth texture and a strong dark chocolate flavor. The key to the flavor is a generous amount of cocoa powder, which has intense chocolate notes.

1½ cups whole milk
¾ cup sugar
¾ cup cocoa powder
1½ cups heavy cream
¼ teaspoon salt
1 teaspoon vanilla extract

1. Whisk together milk, sugar, and cocoa powder in a medium saucepan. Cook over medium heat, stirring to dissolve the sugar and cocoa powder, until mixture comes to a simmer. Remove from heat and stir in cream, salt, and vanilla.

2. Cool to room temperature, then cover and refrigerate until well chilled, 3 to 4 hours, or overnight.

3. Pour chilled mixture into an ice cream maker and freeze as directed.

4. Transfer ice cream to a freezer-safe container and place in the freezer. Allow it to firm up for 1 to 2 hours before serving.

Makes about 1 quart

French-Style Chocolate

This French-style chocolate ice cream is a very rich ice cream that is always a hit with chocolate lovers. The custard-style base is made with egg yolks, which give the finished ice cream a velvety texture and lingering chocolate flavor. Use your favorite dark chocolate in this recipe for the best flavor, though even semisweet chocolate chips will produce a tasty result if you simply want to use what you have in the pantry.

> 1 cup whole milk
> 5 ounces dark chocolate, chopped
> ⅔ cup sugar
> 4 large egg yolks
> 2 cups heavy cream
> 2 teaspoons vanilla extract

1. Combine milk, chocolate, and sugar in a medium saucepan. Cook over medium heat, stirring to dissolve the sugar and the chocolate, until the mixture is smooth and comes to a simmer.

2. Whisk together egg yolks in a large bowl. When the milk mixture comes to a simmer, remove from heat and very slowly stream it into the egg yolk mixture to temper it while whisking constantly. When all the milk mixture has been added, return it to the saucepan and continue to cook over medium heat, stirring constantly, until the mixture has thickened enough to coat the back of a spoon, 2 to 3 minutes. Remove from heat and stir in cream and vanilla.

3. Cool to room temperature, then cover and refrigerate until well chilled, 3 to 4 hours, or overnight.

(continued on next page)

4. Pour chilled mixture into an ice cream maker and freeze as directed.

5. Transfer ice cream to a freezer-safe container and place in the freezer. Allow it to firm up for 1 to 2 hours before serving.

Makes about 1 quart

Milk Chocolate Marshmallow Swirl

As popular as dark chocolate is, milk chocolate can be even more tempting in some dishes. One example of this is in s'mores, where milk chocolate balances with the flavors of the toasted marshmallow and graham crackers better than dark chocolate. This ice cream flavor is s'mores inspired, with a combination of milk chocolate ice cream and a marshmallow swirl, but it leaves out the graham crackers. You can make a s'mores ice cream sandwich, though, with a couple graham crackers and a few scoops of this flavor.

> 1 cup whole milk
> 4 ounces milk chocolate, chopped
> ¾ cup sugar
> 3 large egg yolks
> 2 cups heavy cream
> 1 teaspoon vanilla extract
> 1 (7-ounce) container marshmallow creme or fluff

1. Combine milk, chocolate, and sugar in a medium saucepan. Cook over medium heat, stirring to dissolve the sugar and the chocolate, until the mixture is smooth and comes to a simmer.

2. Whisk together egg yolks in a large bowl. When the milk mixture comes to a simmer, remove from heat and very slowly stream it into the egg yolk mixture to temper it while whisking constantly. When all the milk mixture has been added, return it to the saucepan and continue to cook over medium heat, stirring constantly, until the mixture has thickened enough to coat the back of a spoon, 2 to 3 minutes. Remove from heat and stir in cream and vanilla.

3. Cool to room temperature, then cover and refrigerate until well chilled, 3 to 4 hours, or overnight.

4. Pour chilled mixture into an ice cream maker and freeze as directed. When ice cream has churned, put marshmallow creme in a small, microwave-safe bowl and warm it up for 10 to 15 seconds to give it a more pourable consistency. Fold the softened marshmallow creme into the ice cream as you transfer it to a freezer-safe container to create a swirl.

5. Place ice cream in the freezer and allow it to firm up for 1 to 2 hours before serving.

Makes about 1 quart

Rocky Road

Rocky road is an American classic ice cream flavor created in March 1929 when Joseph Edy and William Dreyer put marshmallows and walnuts into chocolate ice cream. After the Stock Market Crash of 1929, which started the Great Depression, the partners named the flavor rocky road "to give folks something to smile about in the midst of the Great Depression." Miniature marshmallows are the easiest to work with, but if you can't find them, you can use large marshmallows and cut them into halves or quarters with a lightly greased sharp knife.

 1½ cups whole milk
 ¾ cup sugar
 ⅔ cup cocoa powder
 1½ cups heavy cream
 ¼ teaspoon salt
 1 teaspoon vanilla extract
 1½ cups miniature marshmallows
 1 cup toasted walnuts, coarsely chopped

1. Whisk together milk, sugar, and cocoa powder in a medium saucepan. Cook over medium heat, stirring to dissolve the sugar and cocoa powder, until mixture comes to a simmer. Remove from heat and stir in cream, salt, and vanilla.

2. Cool to room temperature, then cover and refrigerate until well chilled, 3 to 4 hours, or overnight.

3. Pour chilled mixture into an ice cream maker and freeze as directed. When ice cream has churned, fold in marshmallows and walnuts.

4. Transfer ice cream to a freezer-safe container and place in the freezer. Allow it to firm up for 1 to 2 hours before serving.

Makes about 1 quart

Chocolate Chip Cookie Dough

This ice cream flavor is popular with anyone who ever snuck a taste of cookie dough out of a bowl their mom was mixing when they were kids. It was first mass-produced by Ben & Jerry's and has been a staple of most ice cream brands for decades. The key is to use an eggless chocolate chip cookie dough that doesn't need to be baked, so that you can get that classic cookie dough flavor and texture in a homemade version of the ice cream.

- 1½ cups whole milk
- ¾ cup sugar
- 2 cups heavy cream
- 2 teaspoons vanilla extract
- 1 cup Chocolate Chip Cookie Dough Chunks (recipe follows)

1. Combine milk and sugar in a medium saucepan. Bring to a simmer, stirring until the sugar is dissolved. Remove from heat and stir in cream and vanilla.

2. Cover and refrigerate until well chilled, 3 to 4 hours, or overnight.

3. Pour chilled mixture into an ice cream maker and freeze as directed.

(continued on next page)

4. When ice cream has churned, fold in the cookie dough chunks to evenly distribute them throughout the ice cream.

5. Transfer ice cream to a freezer-safe container and place in the freezer. Allow it to firm up for 1 to 2 hours before serving.

Makes about 1 quart

Chocolate Chip Cookie Dough Chunks

⅓ cup butter, room temperature
½ cup brown sugar, packed
½ teaspoon vanilla extract
¼ teaspoon salt
 1 tablespoon milk
½ cup all-purpose flour
½ cup mini chocolate chips

1. Cream together butter and sugar until creamy. Blend in the vanilla, salt, and milk. Blend in the flour until dough comes together. Stir in chocolate chips.

2. Roll dough into small, almond-sized balls. Refrigerate until ready to use.

Makes about 1 cup

Mocha Almond Chip

Mocha almond is one of my favorite flavors at a national ice cream chain. Mocha is a good flavor both for coffee drinks and for ice cream, but when you are eating it as ice cream you have the option of adding additional textures to it. Chocolate chips add an extra punch of chocolate, while chopped toasted almonds add some much-needed crunch and highlight the roasted notes of the coffee so that it doesn't get drowned out in all that chocolate.

> 1½ cups whole milk
> ½ cup cocoa powder
> 1½ tablespoons instant coffee or espresso powder
> ¾ cup sugar
> 1½ cups heavy cream
> 1 teaspoon vanilla extract
> 3 ounces dark or semisweet chocolate, coarsely chopped
> 2 teaspoons vegetable oil
> ½ cup toasted almonds, finely chopped

1. Whisk together milk, cocoa powder, instant coffee, and sugar in a medium saucepan. Cook over medium heat, stirring to dissolve the cocoa powder, coffee, and sugar, until mixture comes to a simmer. Remove from heat and stir in cream and vanilla.

2. Cool to room temperature, then cover and refrigerate until well chilled, 3 to 4 hours, or overnight.

3. Pour chilled mixture into an ice cream maker and freeze as directed.

(continued on next page)

4. While ice cream is freezing, combine the chocolate and vegetable oil in a small microwave-safe bowl. Microwave on medium power in 30- to 40-second intervals, stirring regularly, until chocolate is melted and mixture is smooth.

5. When ice cream is churned, drizzle the chocolate mixture into the ice cream as you transfer it into a freezer-safe container, creating ribbons of chocolate that will break up as you stir it gently. Incorporate all of the chocolate mixture, then fold in the almonds. Place ice cream in freezer and allow it to firm up for 1 to 2 hours before serving.

Makes about 1 quart

Coffee

Unlike chocolate and vanilla, coffee ice cream wasn't one of my favorite flavors when I was a kid, but it turned into one as I grew up. Coffee and ice cream are a natural fit, because coffee is often best when it is served with a little bit of cream and sugar. Instant coffee is an easy way to infuse strong coffee flavor into an ice cream base. Instant espresso powder, which is available at specialty stores, is a great way to boost the coffee flavor a little bit more.

1 cup whole milk

2 tablespoons instant coffee or espresso powder

¾ cup sugar

1 large egg

3 large egg yolks

2 cups heavy cream

1 teaspoon vanilla extract

1. Combine milk, instant coffee, and sugar in a large saucepan. Bring to a simmer, stirring until the coffee and sugar are dissolved.

2. Whisk together egg and egg yolks in a large bowl. When the milk mixture comes to a simmer, remove from heat and very slowly stream it into the egg mixture to temper it while whisking constantly. When all the milk mixture has been added, return it to the saucepan and continue to cook over medium heat, stirring constantly, until the mixture has thickened enough to coat the back of a spoon, 2 to 3 minutes. Remove from heat and stir in cream and vanilla.

3. Cover milk mixture and allow to cool to room temperature, then refrigerate until well chilled, 3 to 4 hours, or overnight.

4. Pour chilled mixture into an ice cream maker and freeze as directed.

5. Transfer ice cream to a freezer-safe container and place in the freezer. Allow it to firm up for 1 to 2 hours before serving.

Makes about 1 quart

Buttermilk

The light, tangy flavor of buttermilk can be delicious in ice cream because it adds a slightly tart element to all that cream. The result is an ice cream that tastes lighter and slightly brighter than some other flavors. It pairs extremely well with fresh berries and berry desserts, such as cobblers and pies.

- 2 cups heavy cream
- ¾ cup sugar
- 2 teaspoons vanilla extract
- 1¼ cups buttermilk

1. Combine cream and sugar in a medium saucepan. Bring to a simmer, stirring until the sugar is dissolved. Remove from heat and stir in vanilla. Cover and refrigerate until well chilled, 3 to 4 hours, or overnight. When mixture is thoroughly chilled, stir in buttermilk.

2. Pour buttermilk mixture into an ice cream maker and freeze as directed.

3. Transfer ice cream to a freezer-safe container and place in the freezer. Allow it to firm up for 1 to 2 hours before serving.

Makes about 1 quart

FRUIT AND NUTS

Fresh Strawberry

Fresh strawberries are a summertime treat that people look forward to all year. When they are in season, strawberries are irresistibly sweet — and that flavor translates well into ice cream. Strawberry has been a consistently popular ice cream flavor for years, with no signs of waning. Fresh, in-season strawberries are the best choice for this ice cream, but if you can't find good ones, frozen strawberries that have been completely defrosted can also deliver a good result because they are usually frozen at their peak. Add a few drops of red food coloring to boost the pink color, if desired.

> 16 ounces fresh strawberries, hulled
> ¾ cup sugar
> 1 teaspoon lemon juice
> 2 cups heavy cream
> 1 cup whole milk
> ¼ teaspoon red food coloring (optional)

1. Purée the strawberries, sugar, and lemon juice in a food processor or blender until mixture is completely smooth and sugar is dissolved. Stir in cream, milk, and red food coloring, if using.

2. Cover strawberry mixture and refrigerate until well chilled, 3 to 4 hours, or overnight.

(continued on next page)

3. Pour chilled mixture into an ice cream maker and freeze as directed.

4. Transfer ice cream to a freezer-safe container and place in the freezer. Allow it to firm up for 1 to 2 hours before serving.

Makes about 1 quart

Roasted Fig and Honey

Fresh figs have a lovely jamlike sweetness to them when they are ripe, but you can intensify that sweetness by roasting the fruit. This ice cream is full of tender roasted figs and highlights their honeyed sweetness by pairing them with a honey-sweetened ice cream base.

    8 ounces fresh, ripe black figs
    1 cup whole milk
    ¼ cup honey
    ½ cup sugar
    2 cups heavy cream
    1 teaspoon vanilla extract

1. Preheat the oven to 350°F. Line a baking sheet with parchment paper.

2. Quarter figs and place on prepared baking sheet, cut sides up. Roast for 9 to 12 minutes, or until tender. Set aside to cool to room temperature. If preparing figs in advance, they can be stored overnight in a covered container in the refrigerator.

3. Combine milk, honey, and sugar in a small saucepan. Cook over medium heat, stirring with a spatula, until honey and sugar have dissolved and mixture comes to a simmer. Remove from heat and stir in cream and vanilla.

4. Cover and refrigerate until well chilled, 3 to 4 hours, or overnight.

5. Pour chilled mixture into an ice cream maker and freeze as directed.

6. Once the ice cream base has finished churning, fold in the cooled, roasted figs.

7. Transfer ice cream to a freezer-safe container and place in the freezer. Allow it to firm up for 1 to 2 hours before serving.

Makes about 1 quart

Cherry Vanilla Chip

This version of Ben & Jerry's popular Cherry Garcia is a cherry and vanilla ice cream studded with chunks of chocolate. The chunks of chocolate in here aren't quite the same as the chips in a traditional chocolate chip ice cream. That is because this ice cream is all about the cherries; the chocolate is there to add some crunch to the cherries and only add in a little bit of chocolate flavor. Jarred or frozen and defrosted cherries are the best choice in this recipe because they have a softer texture than fresh cherries and are easily incorporated into the ice cream.

1	cup whole milk
¾	cup sugar
2	cups heavy cream
1	teaspoon vanilla extract
1½	cups halved cherries, jarred or frozen and defrosted
1	cup finely chopped dark chocolate chunks

1. Combine milk and sugar in a medium saucepan. Bring to a simmer, stirring until the sugar is dissolved. Remove from heat and stir in cream and vanilla.

2. Cover and refrigerate until well chilled, 3 to 4 hours, or overnight.

3. Pour chilled mixture into an ice cream maker and freeze as directed.

4. When ice cream is churned, fold in the cherries and dark chocolate chunks.

5. Transfer ice cream to a freezer-safe container and place in the freezer. Allow it to firm up for 1 to 2 hours before serving.

Makes about 1 quart

Peaches and Cream

Peach ice cream is like summer in a cup. Not only does the ice cream have a honeyed sweetness from ripe peaches, but it also has a lovely yellow hue that makes the ice cream look very sunny and bright. Unlike berries, peaches need to be cooked slightly to tenderize them and enhance their sweetness before they can be puréed and incorporated into an ice cream base. If you are feeling adventurous, a mixture of half peaches and half apricots can make a wonderful variation.

16 ounces peaches, peeled and pitted
¾ cup sugar
2 cups heavy cream
1 cup whole milk
1 teaspoon vanilla extract

1. Slice peaches into eighths. Combine peaches and sugar in a medium saucepan and cook over medium heat, stirring to dissolve the sugar. Cook until peaches are tender, about 5 minutes. Remove from heat and allow peaches to cool.

2. Purée the cooled peaches in a food processor or blender until they are completely smooth. Stir in cream, milk, and vanilla.

3. Cover peach mixture and refrigerate until well chilled, 3 to 4 hours, or overnight.

4. Pour chilled mixture into an ice cream maker and freeze as directed.

5. Transfer ice cream to a freezer-safe container and place in the freezer. Allow it to firm up for 1 to 2 hours before serving.

Makes about 1 quart

Toasted Coconut

This coconut ice cream is made with two different forms of coconut: shredded coconut and coconut milk. Coconut milk only has a mild coconut flavor, whereas the sweetened, shredded coconut delivers a lot of coconut flavor — especially after it has been lightly toasted. Because long strands of coconut will take away from the creaminess of the ice cream, make sure to finely chop the coconut before stirring it in.

- 1½ cups sweetened shredded coconut
- 1 cup coconut milk
- ¾ cup sugar
- 2 cups heavy cream
- ¼ teaspoon salt
- 1 teaspoon vanilla extract

1. Place shredded coconut in a large skillet and cook over medium heat, stirring occasionally with a spoon or spatula, until coconut starts to turn golden brown. As it starts to toast, stir the coconut more often so that it browns evenly. When coconut is golden, remove from heat and allow to cool.

2. Finely chop coconut with a sharp knife and set aside.

3. Combine coconut milk and sugar in a medium saucepan. Bring to a simmer, stirring until the sugar is dissolved. Remove from heat and stir in cream, salt, and vanilla.

4. Cover and refrigerate until well chilled, 3 to 4 hours, or overnight.

5. Pour chilled mixture into an ice cream maker and freeze as directed.

6. When ice cream is churned, fold in the toasted coconut. Transfer ice cream to a freezer-safe container and place in the freezer. Allow it to firm up for 1 to 2 hours before serving.

Makes about 1 quart

Blackberry Cobbler

A freshly baked cobbler isn't ready to serve unless you have a pint of vanilla ice cream to plate alongside it. This ice cream flavor combines the cobbler and the ice cream into one delicious dish. You will need to bake a streusel-like crumble topping in advance, but it is worth a few extra minutes of work because it is addictive with or without ice cream and can be used to top a dish of many other flavors, as well.

1½ cups whole milk
¾ cup sugar
2 cups heavy cream
2 teaspoons vanilla extract
1½ cups fresh blackberries, coarsely chopped
2 cups Almond Crumble Topping (recipe follows)

1. Combine milk and sugar in a medium saucepan. Bring to a simmer, stirring until the sugar is dissolved. Remove from heat and stir in cream and vanilla.

(continued on next page)

2. Cover and refrigerate until well chilled, 3 to 4 hours, or overnight.

3. Pour chilled mixture into an ice cream maker and freeze as directed.

4. When ice cream is churned, fold in the blackberries and almond crumble.

5. Transfer ice cream to a freezer-safe container and place in the freezer. Allow it to firm up for 1 to 2 hours before serving.

Makes about 1½ quarts

Almond Crumble Topping

    ½ cup all-purpose flour
    ½ cup sliced or slivered almonds
    ½ cup confectioners' sugar
    ¼ cup brown sugar, packed
    ⅛ teaspoon salt
    ¼ teaspoon ground cinnamon
    4 tablespoons butter, chilled and cut into several pieces

1. Preheat oven to 350°F. Line a baking sheet with parchment paper.

2. Combine flour, almonds, sugars, salt, and cinnamon in a food processor and whiz until almonds are completely broken up into almond meal and the mixture is well combined. Add

butter and pulse until mixture has a coarse, sandy texture and no pieces of butter larger than a pea remain.

3. Transfer mixture to a large bowl. If you squeeze the mixture firmly in your hand, it should stick together in large crumbles ranging from the size of a pea to a walnut. Break up the whole mixture into various sized crumbles.

4. Transfer almond crumbles to the prepared baking sheet.

5. Bake for about 15 minutes, stirring slightly with a spatula every 5 minutes, until the crumble is light golden and crispy. When completely cooled, crumble can be stored for several days in an airtight container.

Makes about 2 cups

Banana Pudding

Banana pudding is another classic American dessert that makes a good transition to ice cream format. The dessert is traditionally made with vanilla pudding and sliced bananas. Here, it is made with a rich vanilla ice cream base that is infused with bananas. Some diced banana is added after the ice cream has churned to give it a little bit of texture. The traditional pudding is served with vanilla wafer cookies, and you can use them to make great mini ice cream sandwiches.

> 1 cup whole milk
> ¾ cup sugar
> 1 large egg
> 3 large egg yolks
> 2 cups heavy cream
> 2 teaspoons vanilla extract
> 3 ripe bananas
> 1 tablespoon lemon juice

1. Combine milk and sugar in a large saucepan. Bring to a simmer, stirring until the sugar is dissolved.

2. Whisk together egg and egg yolks in a large bowl. When the milk mixture comes to a simmer, remove it from the heat and very slowly stream it into the egg mixture to temper it while whisking constantly. When all the milk mixture has been added, return it to the saucepan and continue to cook over medium heat, stirring constantly, until the mixture has thickened enough to coat the back of a spoon, 2 to 3 minutes. Remove from heat and stir in cream and vanilla.

3. Mash two bananas with lemon juice in a medium bowl until puréed (yield about 1 cup). Stir into milk mixture.

4. Cover milk mixture and allow to cool to room temperature, then refrigerate until well chilled, 3 to 4 hours, or overnight.

5. Pour chilled mixture into an ice cream maker and freeze as directed. When ice cream has churned, dice remaining banana into very small pieces and fold into ice cream.

6. Transfer ice cream to a freezer-safe container and place in the freezer. Allow it to firm up for 1 to 2 hours before serving.

Makes about 1½ quarts

Creamy Lemon Curd

Lemon is a refreshing flavor to find in ice cream, reminiscent of lemonade on a hot summer day. Lemon isn't always an easy flavor to incorporate into a milk mixture, however, since acidic lemon juice can actually curdle milk. One solution is to make a zesty homemade lemon curd as a flavor base, which can easily be incorporated into an ice cream recipe and will give the ice cream a vibrant lemon flavor.

  1⅓ cups Lemon Curd (recipe follows), chilled
  ⅓ cup confectioners' sugar
  1 cup whole milk
  1 cup heavy cream

1. Whisk together lemon curd and confectioners' sugar until sugar is dissolved. Stir in milk and cream until completely incorporated. Chill for 1 hour, or until very cold.

2. Pour chilled mixture into an ice cream maker and freeze as directed.

3. Transfer ice cream to a freezer-safe container and place in the freezer. Allow it to firm up for 1 to 2 hours before serving.

Makes about 1 quart

Lemon Curd

⅔ cup strained, fresh lemon juice
10 tablespoons sugar
1 tablespoon fresh lemon zest
2 large eggs, room temperature
1 teaspoon vanilla extract
2 tablespoons butter, slightly softened

1. Combine lemon juice and sugar in a small saucepan over medium heat. Add zest and stir until sugar is dissolved completely.

2. Lightly beat eggs in a medium bowl. Whisking constantly (or with an electric mixer on low), very slowly stream the hot lemon-sugar syrup into the egg. Beat vigorously for 1 to 2 minutes, then transfer back into the saucepan by pouring the mixture through a sieve.

3. Cook over low heat, stirring constantly, until the curd just comes to a boil. Remove from heat and stir in vanilla and butter, stirring until butter is completely incorporated.

4. Transfer to a small airtight container and chill in the refrigerator until cold, 2 to 3 hours.

Makes 1⅓ cups

Chocolate Hazelnut

Chocolate and hazelnuts are a delicious combination, and anyone who has ever eaten a spoonful of Nutella, the popular chocolate hazelnut spread, would agree. This ice cream flavor uses that creamy chocolate spread to infuse both chocolate and hazelnut flavor into a frozen dessert. It's decadent, and delicious, especially when you finish it off with an extra swirl of that same chocolate spread so you get a taste of the ice cream and the spread in every scoop.

1 cup whole milk

¾ cup sugar

⅓ cup cocoa powder

¼ teaspoon salt

1 large egg

3 large egg yolks

1 cup chocolate hazelnut spread, such as Nutella

1 teaspoon vanilla extract

2 cups heavy cream

1. Combine milk, sugar, cocoa powder, and salt in a medium saucepan. Cook over medium heat, stirring to dissolve the sugar and the cocoa powder, until the mixture is smooth and comes to a simmer.

2. Whisk together egg and egg yolks in a large bowl. When the milk mixture comes to a simmer, remove from heat and very slowly stream it into the egg mixture to temper it while whisking constantly. When all the milk mixture has been added, return it to the saucepan and continue to cook over medium heat, stirring constantly, until the mixture has thickened enough to coat the back of a spoon, 2 to 3 minutes. Remove from heat and add ½ cup of the chocolate hazelnut spread and vanilla. Allow mixture to sit for 1 to 2 minutes to melt the hazelnut spread, then whisk until it is completely incorporated. Stir in cream.

3. Cool to room temperature, then cover and refrigerate until well chilled, 3 to 4 hours, or overnight.

4. Pour chilled mixture into an ice cream maker and freeze as directed.

5. In a small, microwave-safe bowl, heat the remaining ½ cup of chocolate hazelnut spread in the microwave for 10 to 20 seconds to soften it. Drizzle the softened spread into the ice cream as you transfer it to a freezer-safe container to create a chocolate hazelnut swirl. Place ice cream in the freezer and allow it to firm up for 1 to 2 hours before serving.

Makes about 1 quart

Butter Pecan

Butter pecan is an addictive ice cream flavor that is a favorite of many, even people who aren't normally big fans of nuts in ice cream. To get the flavor, pecans are toasted in butter in a skillet before being added to the ice cream base. Not only do the nuts get toasted, but they also get infused with butter and become richer and more tender than before. The butter also takes on some of the toasted flavor from the pecans, and that permeates the ice cream in the most delicious way.

        4 tablespoons butter
        1 cup finely chopped pecans
        ¼ teaspoon salt
        1 cup whole milk
        ¾ cup sugar
        1 teaspoon vanilla extract
        2 cups heavy cream

1. Melt the butter over medium heat in a medium skillet. Add pecans and cook, stirring constantly, until pecans are toasted and the butter starts to take on a light golden color, about 3 minutes. Remove from heat, stir in salt, and transfer to a small bowl to cool to room temperature.

2. Combine milk and sugar in a small saucepan and cook over medium heat, stirring until the sugar dissolves. Remove from heat and stir in vanilla and cream.

3. Cover milk mixture and allow to cool to room temperature, then refrigerate until well chilled, 3 to 4 hours, or overnight.

4. Pour chilled mixture into an ice cream maker and freeze as directed. When ice cream has churned, fold in pecan mixture.

5. Transfer ice cream to a freezer-safe container and place in the freezer. Allow it to firm up for 1 to 2 hours before serving.

Makes about 1 quart

Honey Roasted Peanut Butter

Peanut butter may not be quite as popular as vanilla, but it has a huge fan base of loyal peanut butter lovers who look for it every time they go out for ice cream. I enjoy honey roasted peanuts even more than regular peanuts, because they have that salty-sweet flavor that I find addictive. This ice cream uses both honey and peanut butter to capture that flavor, and I like to add in a few finely chopped honey roasted peanuts, too. The nuts give the ice cream a little extra texture, highlight the honey notes in the ice cream, and deliver a little pop of salt in every bite.

1½ cups whole milk
1½ cups heavy cream
  1 cup creamy peanut butter
¼ teaspoon salt
½ cup honey
½ teaspoon vanilla extract
½ cup honey roasted peanuts, finely chopped

1. Whisk together milk, cream, peanut butter, salt, honey, and vanilla in a large bowl until all ingredients are completely incorporated and mixture is very smooth.

(continued on next page)

2. Refrigerate until well chilled, 1 to 2 hours, or overnight.

3. Pour chilled mixture into an ice cream maker and freeze as directed. When ice cream has churned, fold in chopped peanuts.

4. Transfer ice cream to a freezer-safe container and place in the freezer. Allow it to firm up for 1 to 2 hours before serving.

Makes about 1 quart

Pistachio

Pistachio ice cream was never my favorite as a kid because most pistachio ice creams are made with lots of artificial pistachio flavor. Real pistachios bring a much fresher flavor to pistachio ice cream — and you might just find that you like it a lot more than you remember. This ice cream will not have the vibrant green color that most commercial pistachio ice creams have, but you can always stir in a few drops of green food coloring for the sake of nostalgia, if you wish. I finish off the ice cream with a small splash of Amaretto, an almond liqueur, but almond extract can be substituted to keep this recipe alcohol-free.

⅔ cup untoasted, unsalted pistachios

2 cups heavy cream

1½ cups whole milk

¾ cup sugar

1 tablespoon Amaretto or ¼ teaspoon almond extract

¼ teaspoon green food coloring (optional)

1. Coarsely chop the pistachios and put them in a medium saucepan. Place saucepan over medium heat, stirring the pistachios regularly with a spatula until they start to toast, 3 to 5 minutes. Add the cream, milk, and sugar. Bring to a simmer, stirring until the sugar is dissolved. Remove from heat. Stir in Amaretto or almond extract, and green food coloring, if using. Cover and let cool to room temperature.

2. Pour the room-temperature mixture through a strainer to remove all of the pistachios, then discard them. Cover and refrigerate until well chilled, 3 to 4 hours, or overnight.

3. Pour chilled mixture into an ice cream maker and freeze as directed.

4. Transfer ice cream to a freezer-safe container and place in the freezer. Allow it to firm up for 1 to 2 hours before serving.

Makes about 1 quart

SUGAR AND SPICE

Honey and Vanilla Bean

Honey is an ingredient that doesn't always get much time in the spotlight. This natural sweetener has a tremendous amount of flavor, and this ice cream is one place that it gets to shine. It is the only sweetener in this ice cream base, and it comes through clearly in every bite, with a little bit of vanilla to round out the flavor of the honey and the cream.

2 cups heavy cream
1 cup whole milk
⅔ cup honey
1 vanilla bean
1 large egg
3 large egg yolks

1. Combine cream, milk, and honey in a large saucepan. Split the vanilla bean lengthwise down the center and add it to the milk mixture. Bring to a simmer, stirring until the honey is dissolved. Remove from heat. Cover and let cool to room temperature. Remove vanilla bean and set aside.

2. Bring milk mixture back up to a simmer.

3. Whisk together egg and egg yolks in a large bowl. When the milk mixture comes to a simmer, remove from heat and very slowly stream it into the egg mixture to temper it while whisking constantly. When all the milk mixture has been added, return it to the saucepan and continue to cook over medium heat, stirring constantly, until the mixture has thickened enough to coat the back of a spoon, 2 to 3 minutes. Remove from heat.

4. With the back of a knife, scrape the vanilla seeds out of the pod you used to infuse the milk. Add the seeds to the cream mixture and discard the pod, or set aside for another use.

5. Cover milk mixture and allow to cool to room temperature, then refrigerate until well chilled, 3 to 4 hours, or overnight.

6. Pour chilled mixture into an ice cream maker and freeze as directed.

7. Transfer ice cream to a freezer-safe container and place in the freezer. Allow it to firm up for 1 to 2 hours before serving.

Makes about 1 quart

Cinnamon Spice

Cinnamon ice cream is almost as versatile as plain vanilla ice cream. It makes wonderful ice cream sandwiches and can be the perfect complement to a slice of pie — especially if that pie already involves a little bit of cinnamon or spice. The method of infusing cinnamon used in this ice cream can also be used with other spices, such as cloves, star anise, or cardamom.

    1½ cups heavy cream
    1½ cups whole milk
    ⅔ cup sugar
    3 (2- to 3-inch-long) cinnamon sticks
    1 vanilla bean
    1 large egg
    3 large egg yolks

1. Combine cream, milk, and sugar in a large saucepan. Add the cinnamon sticks to the milk mixture. Split the vanilla bean lengthwise down the center and add it to the milk mixture. Bring to a simmer, stirring until the sugar is dissolved. Remove from heat. Cover and let cool to room temperature. Remove cinnamon sticks and vanilla bean. Set vanilla bean aside.

2. Bring milk mixture back up to a simmer.

3. Whisk together egg and egg yolks in a large bowl. When the milk mixture comes to a simmer, remove it from the heat and very slowly stream it into the egg mixture to temper it while whisking constantly. When all the milk mixture has been added, return it to the saucepan and continue to cook over medium heat, stirring constantly, until the mixture has thickened enough to coat the back of a spoon, 2 to 3 minutes. Remove from heat.

4. With the back of a knife, scrape the vanilla seeds out of the pod you used to infuse the milk. Add the seeds to the cream mixture and discard the pod, or set aside for another use.

5. Cover milk mixture and allow to cool to room temperature, then refrigerate until well chilled, 3 to 4 hours, or overnight.

6. Pour chilled mixture into an ice cream maker and freeze as directed.

7. Transfer ice cream to a freezer-safe container and place in the freezer. Allow it to firm up for 1 to 2 hours before serving.

Makes about 1 quart

Peppermint Chocolate Chip

Mint chocolate chip ice cream always has a slightly green tint to it. This is partly because fresh mint is a beautiful bright green, but it is also to set it apart from chocolate chip ice cream, so that you don't reach for one and get the other by mistake. The green food coloring is optional, but fans of mint chocolate chip ice cream will appreciate that familiar light green color in their ice cream as they serve themselves a scoop or two of this flavor.

> 1½ cups whole milk
> ¾ cup sugar
> 2 cups heavy cream
> 1 teaspoon vanilla extract
> 1 teaspoon peppermint extract
> 5–6 drops green food coloring (optional)
> 3 ounces dark or semisweet chocolate, coarsely chopped
> 2 teaspoons vegetable oil

1. Combine milk and sugar in a medium saucepan. Bring to a simmer, stirring until the sugar is dissolved. Remove from heat and stir in cream, vanilla, peppermint, and green food coloring, if using.

2. Cover and refrigerate until well chilled, 3 to 4 hours, or overnight.

3. Pour chilled mixture into an ice cream maker and freeze as directed.

4. While ice cream is freezing, combine the chocolate and vegetable oil in a small microwave-safe bowl. Microwave on medium power in 30- to 40-second intervals, stirring regularly until chocolate is melted and mixture is smooth.

5. When ice cream is churned, drizzle the chocolate mixture into the ice cream as you transfer it to a freezer-safe container, creating ribbons of chocolate that will break up as you stir it gently. Incorporate all of the chocolate mixture. Place ice cream in freezer and allow it to firm up for 1 to 2 hours before serving.

Makes about 1 quart

Brown Sugar and Cinnamon

I use brown sugar all the time when baking cookies and cakes, where it adds a hint of molasses flavor to a recipe and often adds some extra moisture to the finished product. Brown sugar brings that same hint of molasses into this simple ice cream. Complemented with a hint of cinnamon the warm old-fashioned flavor, reminds me of fall and winter baking any time of year I eat it.

1½ cups whole milk
¾ cup brown sugar, packed
1 teaspoon ground cinnamon
2 cups heavy cream
2 teaspoons vanilla extract

(continued on next page)

1. Combine milk, brown sugar, and cinnamon in a medium saucepan. Bring to a simmer, stirring until the sugar is dissolved. Remove from heat and stir in cream and vanilla.

2. Cover and refrigerate until well chilled, 3 to 4 hours, or overnight.

3. Pour chilled mixture into an ice cream maker and freeze as directed.

4. Transfer ice cream to a freezer-safe container and allow it to firm up for 1 to 2 hours before serving.

Makes about 1 quart

Butterscotch

Butterscotch sauce was one of my favorite ice cream toppings as a kid, but I later discovered that butterscotch-flavored ice cream is much more delicious than any store-bought topping. In its simplest form, butterscotch is a mixture of butter and brown sugar that is cooked together. It's not quite caramel, because you can really taste the two flavor elements on their own, but it is delicious. This ice cream uses those two flavors as a base, adding a splash of vanilla and a little bourbon to make it a bit more sophisticated. The bourbon can be omitted for an alcohol-free variation.

1 cup brown sugar, packed
4 tablespoons butter
¼ teaspoon salt
1 cup whole milk

1 large egg
3 large egg yolks
1 teaspoon vanilla extract
1 tablespoon bourbon
2 cups heavy cream

1. Combine the sugar, butter, and salt in a large saucepan. Cook over medium heat, stirring until the sugar completely dissolves and the mixture begins to simmer. Add in the milk and bring the mixture back up to a simmer.

2. Whisk together egg and egg yolks in a large bowl. When the milk mixture comes to a simmer, remove from heat and very slowly stream it into the egg mixture to temper it while whisking constantly. When all the milk mixture has been added, return it to the saucepan and continue to cook over medium heat, stirring constantly, until the mixture has thickened enough to coat the back of a spoon, 2 to 3 minutes. Remove from heat. Whisk in vanilla, bourbon, and cream.

3. Cover milk mixture and allow to cool to room temperature, then refrigerate until well chilled, 3 to 4 hours, or overnight.

4. Pour chilled mixture into an ice cream maker and freeze as directed.

5. Transfer ice cream to a freezer-safe container and place in the freezer. Allow it to firm up for 1 to 2 hours before serving.

Makes about 1 quart

Fresh Ginger

Sweet and spicy, this ginger ice cream has a refreshing and addictive quality that will make you want to eat it again and again. Fresh ginger root is the key to getting a great flavor in this ice cream, because it is much more potent than dried ginger. Once the ice cream base is infused, you will need to strain out the remaining ginger pieces because they are fibrous and not something you will want to find in your finished ice cream.

- 2 cups heavy cream
- 1 cup whole milk
- ¾ cup sugar
- 1 (3-inch) piece fresh ginger root, peeled and coarsely chopped
- 1 large egg
- 3 large egg yolks
- 1 teaspoon vanilla extract

1. Combine cream, milk, sugar, and ginger in a large saucepan. Bring to a simmer, stirring until the sugar is dissolved. Remove from heat. Cover and let cool to room temperature. Strain the mixture to remove all of the ginger root.

2. Bring milk mixture back up to a simmer.

3. Whisk together egg and egg yolks in a large bowl. When the milk mixture comes to a simmer, remove from heat and very slowly stream it into the egg mixture to temper it while whisking constantly. When all the milk mixture has been added, return it to the saucepan and continue to cook

on medium heat, stirring constantly, until the mixture has thickened enough to coat the back of a spoon, 2 to 3 minutes. Remove from heat and whisk in vanilla.

4. Cover milk mixture and allow to cool to room temperature, then refrigerate until well chilled, 3 to 4 hours, or overnight.

5. Pour chilled mixture into an ice cream maker and freeze as directed.

6. Transfer ice cream to a freezer-safe container and place in the freezer. Allow it to firm up for 1 to 2 hours before serving.

Makes about 1 quart

GOURMET

Chocolate Cereal Milk

Cereal milk is the sweetened milk that is left over at the bottom of a bowl of sugary cereal. It's a flavor that is sure to transport you back to watching cartoons on a lazy Saturday morning when you were a kid, and, although it may sound strange, it has the same transporting effect as an ice cream flavor, as well. This recipe starts with chocolate breakfast cereal, which produces a delicious chocolate milk–flavored ice cream.

> 2 cups heavy cream
> 1 cup whole milk
> 2 cups chocolate breakfast cereal, such as Cocoa Krispies
> ½ cup sugar

1. Combine 1 cup of the cream with the milk and cereal in a large bowl. Stir to coat the cereal with the milk mixture, then cover with plastic wrap and allow mixture to stand at room temperature for 2 hours to infuse the milk mixture. Strain out cereal through a fine-mesh strainer, gently pressing the leftover cereal with a spatula to remove excess liquid. You should have approximately 1¼ cups liquid after straining.

2. Stir sugar into strained cereal milk and whisk until it dissolves. Stir in the remaining 1 cup cream. Refrigerate until well chilled, 1 to 2 hours.

3. Pour chilled mixture into an ice cream maker and freeze as directed.

4. Transfer ice cream to a freezer-safe container and place in the freezer. Allow it to firm up for 1 to 2 hours before serving.

Makes about 1 quart

Browned Butter

Browned butter is like a secret weapon in the kitchen. It is made by cooking butter over medium heat until the milk solids in it start to caramelize and take on a nutty, toasted flavor. It's subtle but addictive. It makes a great addition to all kinds of dishes, both sweet and savory, and this ice cream is a perfect example of how delicious it can be in desserts.

- 4 tablespoons butter
- ¾ cup sugar
- 2 cups whole milk
- 1 cup heavy cream
- 1½ teaspoons vanilla extract

1. Place butter in a medium saucepan and cook over medium heat until the butter comes to a boil. After 3 to 4 minutes, the butter will start to brown and smell nutty. Stir the butter as it starts to brown to prevent it from burning and scrape the brown bits off the bottom of the pan.

2. When the butter is a dark golden color, add in the sugar and milk. Cook, stirring, until the sugar dissolves and the mixture comes to a simmer. Remove from heat and stir in cream and vanilla.

3. Cool to room temperature, then cover and refrigerate until well chilled, 3 to 4 hours, or overnight.

4. Pour chilled mixture into an ice cream maker and freeze as directed.

5. Transfer ice cream to a freezer-safe container and place in the freezer. Allow it to firm up for 1 to 2 hours before serving.

Makes about 1 quart

Salted Caramel

Salted caramel brings together salty and sweet elements to produce something that is more delicious than the components would be on their own. You might never go back to salted caramel as an ice cream topping alone after a few bites of this dessert.

- ⅓ cup water
- 1 cup sugar
- 1¾ cups heavy cream
- ½ teaspoon salt
- 1½ cups whole milk
- 1 teaspoon vanilla extract

1. Combine water and sugar in a medium saucepan and cook over medium heat, stirring with a spatula just until the sugar dissolves. Bring sugar syrup to a boil and cook until it turns a dark amber color, 3 to 5 minutes.

2. Pour ¾ cup of the cream into the hot caramel. Mixture will bubble vigorously. Add in salt and stir until sauce is smooth. Remove from heat. Add the remaining cream, milk, and vanilla, then stir until mixture is very smooth.

3. Cool to room temperature, then cover and refrigerate until well chilled, 3 to 4 hours, or overnight.

4. Pour chilled mixture into an ice cream maker and freeze as directed.

5. Transfer ice cream to a freezer-safe container and place in the freezer. Allow it to firm up for 1 to 2 hours before serving.

Makes about 1 quart

Dulce de Leche

Dulce de leche is a very sweet, thick, milk-based caramel sauce that has a strong dairy flavor similar to sweetened condensed milk. It is popular in South American countries, but it is becoming well-known in the United States and elsewhere in the world, so it is now easy to find at most grocery stores. Because of the dairy notes already in the dulce de leche, it makes a great flavor base for ice cream.

1½ cups whole milk
1 (14-ounce) can dulce de leche
2 teaspoons vanilla extract
1½ cups heavy cream

1. Combine the milk, dulce de leche, and vanilla in a medium saucepan. Cook over medium heat, stirring with a spatula or whisk, until dulce de leche is completely dissolved. Remove from heat and stir in cream.

2. Cool to room temperature, then cover and refrigerate until well chilled, 3 to 4 hours, or overnight.

3. Pour chilled mixture into an ice cream maker and freeze as directed.

4. Transfer to a freezer-safe container and allow ice cream to firm up for 1 to 2 hours before serving.

Makes about 1 quart

Matcha

Matcha is a brightly colored, finely milled green tea powder that is popular in many culinary applications, in addition to tea preparations, because of its bold color and its distinctive slightly bitter flavor. It produces a bright green ice cream that is more refreshing than sweet. It's a great contrast to a spicy meal.

   1 cup whole milk
   ¾ cup sugar
   4 tablespoons matcha powder
   2 cups heavy cream

1. Combine milk, sugar, and matcha in a medium saucepan and whisk until matcha powder is dissolved. Bring to a simmer over medium heat, whisking until sugar is dissolved. Remove from heat and stir in cream.

2. Cool to room temperature, then cover and refrigerate until well chilled, 3 to 4 hours, or overnight.

3. Pour chilled mixture into an ice cream maker and freeze as directed.

4. Transfer ice cream to a freezer-safe container and place in the freezer. Allow it to firm up for 1 to 2 hours before serving.

Makes about 1 quart

Maple Bacon

This is another ice cream with addictive sweet and salty elements. The base is a maple syrup ice cream that is delicious on its own, and it is studded with small pieces of crisp, salty bacon bits. It's like having breakfast for dessert — but better. Choose Grade B or Dark Amber maple syrup, rather than a light-colored syrup, for ice cream with a strong, rich maple flavor.

- 2 cups whole milk
- ½ cup heavy cream
- 1 cup maple syrup
- 1 large egg
- 3 large egg yolks
- 1 teaspoon vanilla extract
- 3 ounces bacon, finely chopped

1. Bring milk and cream just to a simmer in a medium saucepan.

2. Whisk together maple syrup, egg, and egg yolks in a large bowl. When milk comes to a simmer, remove from heat and slowly drizzle it into the egg mixture while whisking constantly until all of the milk has been added.

3. Transfer the mixture back to the saucepan and cook over medium heat, stirring constantly until it thickens just enough to coat the back of a spoon. Remove from heat and stir in vanilla.

4. Cool to room temperature, then cover and refrigerate until well chilled, 3 to 4 hours, or overnight.

5. Meanwhile, cook finely chopped bacon in a skillet until very crispy. Drain on a plate lined with paper towels and allow to cool completely.

6. Pour chilled mixture into an ice cream maker and freeze as directed.

7. Fold in bacon bits, then transfer to a freezer-safe container. Place in freezer and allow ice cream to firm up for 1 to 2 hours before serving.

Makes about 1 quart

Cheesecake

Cheesecake is a classic dessert known for its rich, decadent texture, not unlike ice cream. This ice cream takes the flavors of cheesecake and transforms them into a colder and even more indulgent format. The ice cream is made with real cream cheese so it has the same tang as a cheesecake, and it features a sweet graham cracker swirl. Like cheesecake, you can eat this as-is or top it with fresh berries.

     1 cup graham cracker crumbs
     2 tablespoons butter, melted
     1 tablespoon brown sugar, packed
     1 (8-ounce) package cream cheese, room temperature
    ⅔ cup sugar
    1½ cups whole milk
     1 cup heavy cream
     1 teaspoon vanilla extract

1. Preheat oven to 350°F. Line a baking sheet with parchment paper.

2. Stir together graham cracker crumbs, melted butter, and brown sugar in a small bowl. Mixture should be crumbly. Transfer to prepared baking sheet and bake for 10 to 14 minutes, until golden brown and crisp. Allow to cool completely, then store in an airtight container until ready to use.

3. Beat together cream cheese and sugar in a large bowl until sugar is dissolved. Slowly blend in milk, cream, and vanilla until mixture is very smooth.

4. Cover and refrigerate until well chilled, 3 to 4 hours, or overnight.

5. Pour chilled mixture into an ice cream maker and freeze as directed.

6. Transfer to a freezer-safe container and stir in graham cracker mixture with a spatula to create a swirl. Place ice cream in freezer and allow it to firm up for 1 to 2 hours before serving.

Makes about 1 quart

Goat Cheese and Honey

The creamy texture and tangy flavor of goat cheese are two reasons why it is so delicious. Goat cheese is often incorporated into savory dishes, but the creamy cheese can be as versatile as cream cheese and makes a lovely addition to desserts. In this simple recipe, the sweet honey really complements the tang of the goat cheese. Serve it with fresh berries and an extra drizzle of honey for a fantastic summer dessert.

> 1 cup whole milk
> ¼ cup honey
> ½ cup sugar
> 4 ounces goat cheese, room temperature
> 1 teaspoon vanilla extract
> 1¾ cups heavy cream

1. Combine milk, honey, and sugar in a small saucepan. Cook over medium heat, stirring with a spatula, until honey and sugar have dissolved and mixture comes to a simmer.

(continued on next page)

2. Crumble goat cheese and vanilla together in a medium bowl. Pour hot milk mixture over the goat cheese and allow mixture to stand until the goat cheese is slightly melted, 2 to 3 minutes. Gently whisk until goat cheese is dissolved. Pour in the cream.

3. Cover and refrigerate until well chilled, 3 to 4 hours, or overnight.

4. Pour chilled mixture into an ice cream maker and freeze as directed.

5. Transfer ice cream to a freezer-safe container and place in the freezer. Allow it to firm up for 1 to 2 hours before serving.

Makes about 1 quart

Root Beer Float

Root beer floats were one of my favorite treats as a kid. The combination of spicy, fizzy soda and sweet vanilla ice cream was impossible to resist. This ice cream combines both of those elements into one scoop of ice cream that has vanilla and spice notes to it. It starts by concentrating root beer into an intense syrup to flavor the ice cream. Start with a brand that you like, because that is what you'll taste in the finished ice cream. And feel free to double up on the root beer in your next float by topping a few scoops of this with a generous pour of soda.

- 1 (24-ounce) bottle root beer (not diet)
- ¼ cup sugar
- 1 teaspoon vanilla extract
- 1 cup whole milk
- 2 cups heavy cream

1. Bring the root beer to a simmer in a small saucepan over medium heat and reduce it from 24 ounces to 6 ounces, or about ¾ cup, about 20 minutes. Remove from heat and add in sugar and vanilla, stirring until sugar dissolves.

2. Combine root beer syrup with milk and cream.

3. Cool to room temperature, then cover and refrigerate until well chilled, 3 to 4 hours, or overnight.

4. Pour chilled mixture into an ice cream maker and freeze as directed.

5. Transfer ice cream to a freezer-safe container and place in the freezer. Allow it to firm up for 1 to 2 hours before serving.

Makes about 1 quart

HOLIDAY

Eggnog

Eggnog is a nutmeg-laced drink that has been popular during the holidays for well over a century. It is made with milk, eggs, and sugar, which makes the drink a natural fit for an ice cream recipe. Traditionally, eggnog is spiked with a little bit of brandy, bourbon, or rum, but that can be omitted in this recipe for a nonalcoholic, family-friendly frozen dessert.

- 1½ cups whole milk
- ¾ cup sugar
- ¼ teaspoon freshly grated nutmeg
- 2 large eggs
- 4 large egg yolks
- 1½ cups heavy cream
- 2 teaspoons vanilla extract
- 2 ounces bourbon or brandy (optional)

1. Combine milk, sugar, and nutmeg in a medium saucepan. Cook over medium heat, stirring to dissolve the sugar, until mixture comes to a simmer.

2. Whisk together eggs and egg yolks in a large bowl. When the milk mixture comes to a simmer, remove from heat and very slowly stream it into the egg mixture to temper it while whisking constantly. When all the milk mixture has been added, return it to the saucepan and continue to cook over medium heat, stirring constantly, until the mixture has thickened enough to coat the back of a spoon, 2 to 3 minutes. Remove from heat and stir in the cream, vanilla, and bourbon, if using.

3. Cool milk mixture to room temperature, then cover and refrigerate until well chilled, 3 to 4 hours, or overnight.

4. Pour chilled mixture into an ice cream maker and freeze as directed.

5. Transfer ice cream to a freezer-safe container and place in the freezer. Allow it to firm up for 1 to 2 hours before serving.

Makes about 1 quart

Irish Coffee

Irish coffee is made by sweetening strong coffee with a little brown sugar, adding a splash of whiskey, and floating a thick layer of cream on top. You get just the right amount of each element as you sip this classic drink, which rose to popularity in the early 1950s, and you'll get all of those flavors in this whiskey-laced ice cream version. It also makes a wonderful after-dinner drink if you serve it affogato-style, placing a scoop in a coffee cup and pouring a little hot coffee over it before serving.

> 1 cup whole milk
> 1½ tablespoons instant coffee or espresso powder
> ⅔ cup brown sugar, packed
> 1 large egg
> 3 large egg yolks
> ¼ cup Irish whiskey
> ½ teaspoon vanilla extract
> 2 cups heavy cream

1. Combine milk, instant coffee, and sugar in a medium saucepan. Cook over medium heat, stirring to dissolve the sugar, until mixture comes to a simmer.

2. Whisk together egg and egg yolks in a large bowl. When the milk mixture comes to a simmer, remove from heat and very slowly stream it into the egg mixture to temper it while whisking constantly. When all the milk mixture has been added, return it to the saucepan and continue to cook over medium heat, stirring constantly, until the mixture has thickened enough to coat the back of a spoon, 2 to 3 minutes. Remove from heat and stir in whiskey, vanilla, and cream.

3. Cool milk mixture to room temperature, then cover and refrigerate until well chilled, 3 to 4 hours, or overnight.

4. Pour chilled mixture into an ice cream maker and freeze as directed.

5. Transfer ice cream to a freezer-safe container and place in the freezer. Allow it to firm up for 1 to 2 hours before serving.

Makes about 1 quart

Gingerbread Cookie

Brown sugar, molasses, and ginger are the flavors that make up the sweet, spicy flavor of gingerbread, and they give that same flavor profile to this ice cream. It is a wonderful holiday dessert and makes fantastic ice cream sandwiches if you happen to have some real gingerbread cookies in your pantry.

1¼ cups whole milk
3 tablespoons molasses
½ cup brown sugar, packed
1½ teaspoons ground cinnamon
1 teaspoon vanilla extract
2 cups heavy cream
½ cup finely chopped candied ginger

1. Combine milk, molasses, sugar, and cinnamon in a medium saucepan. Cook over medium heat, stirring to dissolve the sugar, until mixture comes to a simmer. Remove from heat and stir in vanilla and cream.

2. Cool to room temperature, then cover and refrigerate until well chilled, 3 to 4 hours, or overnight.

3. Pour chilled mixture into an ice cream maker and freeze as directed.

4. Transfer to a freezer-safe container and stir in candied ginger. Place in freezer and allow ice cream to firm up for 1 to 2 hours before serving.

Makes about 1 quart

Pumpkin Pie

Pumpkin pie is a fall favorite that some people wait all year to eat. This ice cream is something that will remind you of pie, but it is also something that you can enjoy all year long. It really captures the flavor of pumpkin pie, thanks to the addition of pumpkin purée, brown sugar, and pumpkin pie spices. It is excellent as is, but throwing in a handful of chopped, toasted pecans adds a nice crunch and a nutty flavor that goes very well with pumpkin.

2	cups heavy cream
1½	cups whole milk
¾	cup brown sugar, packed
1¼	teaspoons ground cinnamon
½	teaspoon ground ginger
¼	teaspoon ground cloves
1	cup pumpkin purée
3	large egg yolks
1	teaspoon vanilla extract
½	cup chopped , toasted pecans (optional)

1. Combine cream, milk, sugar, cinnamon, ginger, and cloves in a medium saucepan. Cook over medium heat, stirring occasionally, until mixture almost comes to a boil and all of the sugar is dissolved.

2. Meanwhile, whisk together pumpkin purée and egg yolks in a large mixing bowl. When the milk mixture has just about come to a boil, slowly drizzle it into the egg yolk mixture while

(continued on next page)

whisking constantly to temper the eggs. Once the hot cream has been completely incorporated, transfer the mixture back to the saucepan. Cook over medium heat, stirring frequently with a spatula and scraping the bottom and sides of the bowl, until mixture has thickened, about 2 minutes, and coats the back of a spoon. Stir in vanilla and remove from heat.

3. Strain into a large, clean bowl, cover with plastic wrap, and refrigerate until well chilled, 3 to 4 hours or overnight.

4. Pour chilled mixture into an ice cream maker and freeze as directed.

5. Transfer ice cream to a freezer-safe container and place in the freezer. Allow it to firm up for 1 to 2 hours before serving.

Makes about 1½ quarts

Apple Pie à la Mode

Apple pie is best served with a generous scoop of vanilla ice cream on the side. This recipe puts the flavor of apple pie right into the ice cream — no piecrust necessary. Apple cider is reduced down to a thick, syrupy consistency, concentrated enough to infuse a lot of apple flavor into every bite of ice cream. Like vanilla ice cream, this flavor is also delicious when served with a slice of warm apple pie.

> 2 cups apple cider
> ½ cup brown sugar, packed
> ¼ cup granulated sugar
> ½ teaspoon ground cinnamon
> ¼ teaspoon ground allspice
> ¼ teaspoon ground ginger
> 1 teaspoon vanilla extract
> 1 cup whole milk
> 2 cups heavy cream

1. Bring the cider to a simmer in a small saucepan over medium heat and reduce it down to ½ cup, about 20 minutes. Remove from heat and add brown sugar, granulated sugar, cinnamon, allspice, ginger, and vanilla, stirring until sugar dissolves.

2. Combine apple cider syrup with milk and cream.

3. Cool to room temperature, then cover and refrigerate until well chilled, 3 to 4 hours, or overnight.

(continued on next page)

4. Pour chilled mixture into an ice cream maker and freeze as directed.

5. Transfer ice cream to a freezer-safe container and place in the freezer. Allow it to firm up for 1 to 2 hours before serving.

Makes about 1 quart

Peppermint Mocha

Peppermint mocha lattes are one of the most popular holiday drinks at coffee shops all over the country. That kiss of peppermint infuses just the right amount of holiday spirit into what would otherwise be an ordinary drink. Peppermint mochas are typically enjoyed hot, but they are just as delicious cold — and this ice cream version can be served with a dollop of whipped cream and a drizzle of chocolate syrup, just like the coffee shop drink.

1½ cups whole milk

½ cup cocoa powder

1½ tablespoons instant coffee

¾ cup sugar

1½ cups heavy cream

¼ teaspoon salt

1 teaspoon peppermint extract

1 teaspoon vanilla extract

1. Whisk together milk, cocoa powder, instant coffee, and sugar in a medium saucepan. Cook over medium heat, stirring to dissolve the sugar, cocoa powder, and coffee, until mixture comes to a simmer. Remove from heat and stir in cream, salt, peppermint, and vanilla.

2. Cool to room temperature, then cover and refrigerate until well chilled, 3 to 4 hours, or overnight.

3. Pour chilled mixture into an ice cream maker and freeze as directed.

4. Transfer ice cream to a freezer-safe container and place in the freezer. Allow it to firm up for 1 to 2 hours before serving.

Makes about 1 quart

PART THREE

NO-CHURN ICE CREAM RECIPES

You don't need an ice cream maker to make ice cream, and these recipes prove it. At their base, they all have the secret ingredient of sweetened condensed milk — a very sweet canned milk that contains a high proportion of sugar and very little water. This allows it to make an ice cream base that is sweet and surprisingly creamy, because the low water content doesn't allow for ice crystals to form as it freezes. The ice creams are all aerated with whipped cream, rather than with the churning of an ice cream maker. You'll still have to wait for them to set up in your freezer, but you won't need any special equipment to make these recipes.

No-Churn Vanilla

This is one of the easiest ice creams that you can make, and no one would guess that you didn't use an ice cream maker. It has just three ingredients — sweetened condensed milk, heavy whipping cream, and vanilla extract — and takes only a minute or two to put a batch together. If you want the look of vanilla bean ice cream, you can scrape in some vanilla bean seeds before freezing the base.

- 1 (14-ounce) can sweetened condensed milk
- 2 teaspoons vanilla extract
- 2 cups heavy whipping cream

1. Whisk together sweetened condensed milk and vanilla in a large bowl.

2. Whip cream to soft peaks in a medium bowl. Fold into sweetened condensed milk mixture and transfer to a freezer-safe container or loaf pan. Cover with plastic wrap and freeze until firm, at least 3 to 4 hours.

Makes about 1 quart

No-Churn Chocolate

Chocolate lovers will appreciate this easy-to-make chocolate ice cream, although the mousselike ice cream base is so tasty on its own that you might find yourself digging in before it is frozen!

 3 ounces dark or semisweet chocolate
 1 tablespoon unsweetened cocoa powder
 1 (14-ounce) can sweetened condensed milk
 2 teaspoons vanilla extract
 2 cups heavy whipping cream

1. Place chocolate in a small microwave-safe bowl. Microwave it in 45- to 60-second intervals, stirring regularly, to ensure the chocolate doesn't burn. Add in cocoa powder and whisk to combine.

2. Whisk together chocolate mixture, sweetened condensed milk, and vanilla in a large bowl.

3. Whip cream to soft peaks in a medium bowl. Fold into sweetened condensed milk mixture and transfer to a freezer-safe container or loaf pan. Cover with plastic wrap and freeze until firm, at least 3 to 4 hours.

Makes about 1 quart

No-Churn Key Lime Pie

A classic key lime pie is made with sweetened condensed milk in the filling, and so this no-churn ice cream is a natural fit for a frozen version of this wonderful summertime dessert. Fresh lime juice is essential for getting a good lime flavor into the ice cream. Key limes have a sharper, tarter flavor than regular limes and will add the most flavor, but regular lime juice can be substituted and still give you good results.

> 1 (14-ounce) can sweetened condensed milk
> ½ cup freshly squeezed lime juice
> 2 teaspoons finely chopped fresh lime zest
> ½ teaspoon vanilla extract
> 1½ cups heavy whipping cream

1. Whisk together sweetened condensed milk, lime juice, lime zest, and vanilla in a large bowl.

2. Whip cream to soft peaks in a medium bowl. Fold into sweetened condensed milk mixture and transfer to a freezer-safe container or loaf pan. Cover with plastic wrap and freeze until firm, at least 3 to 4 hours.

Makes about 1 quart

No-Churn Butter Pecan

Butter pecan ice cream is a guilty pleasure for many people, and you may find yourself indulging a little bit more often with this easy recipe. The buttery toasted pecans are so delicious that you might want to mix up a second batch to save for topping your ice cream when it is ready to serve!

- 4 tablespoons butter
- 1 cup finely chopped pecans
- ¼ teaspoon salt
- 1 (14-ounce) can sweetened condensed milk
- 2 teaspoons vanilla extract
- 2 cups heavy whipping cream

1. Melt the butter in a medium skillet over medium heat. Add pecans and cook, stirring constantly, until pecans are toasted and the butter starts to take on a light golden color, about 3 minutes. Remove from heat, stir in salt, and transfer to a small bowl to cool to room temperature.

2. Stir pecan mixture into a large bowl with the sweetened condensed milk and vanilla.

3. Whip cream to soft peaks in a medium bowl. Fold into sweetened condensed milk mixture and transfer to a freezer-safe container or loaf pan. Cover with plastic wrap and freeze until firm, at least 3 to 4 hours.

Makes about 1 quart

No-Churn Strawberry

Strawberry ice cream is a classic that never goes out of style, and it can also be made into a tasty no-churn version. You can start with either fresh or frozen strawberries for this recipe, but fresh and in-season fruit will typically give you the best results. Frozen strawberries should be defrosted before you use them. The finished ice cream will have a subtle pink color that isn't as vibrant as store-bought strawberry ice creams. You can add a few drops of red food coloring to boost the color, if desired.

8 ounces strawberries, fresh or frozen and defrosted
1 (14-ounce) can sweetened condensed milk
1 teaspoon vanilla extract
¼ teaspoon red food coloring (optional)
2 cups heavy whipping cream

1. Blend strawberries in a food processor or blender until puréed.

2. Stir together the strawberries, sweetened condensed milk, and vanilla in a large bowl. Stir in red food coloring, if using.

3. Whip cream to soft peaks in a medium bowl. Fold into sweetened condensed milk mixture and transfer to a freezer-safe container or loaf pan. Cover with plastic wrap and freeze until firm, at least 3 to 4 hours.

Makes about 1 quart

No-Churn Cherry Garcia

This version of the popular Ben & Jerry's ice cream flavor couldn't be any easier to make, and it captures those same flavors and textures that you'll find in the packaged version, with plenty of vanilla, chocolate, and cherries. You can use any kind of sweet, dark cherries in this recipe. If cherries are in season, fresh, pitted cherries will add a bright cherry flavor. Otherwise, you can use drained, jarred cherries (not cherry pie filling) or cherries that have been frozen and defrosted.

> 1 (14-ounce) can sweetened condensed milk
>
> 2 teaspoons vanilla extract
>
> 2 cups heavy whipping cream
>
> 2 cups halved sweet cherries, fresh, jarred, or frozen and defrosted
>
> 4 ounces dark chocolate, finely chopped

1. Whisk together sweetened condensed milk and vanilla in a large bowl.

2. Whip cream to soft peaks in a medium bowl. Fold into sweetened condensed milk mixture. Fold in cherries and chopped

dark chocolate, then transfer ice cream to a freezer-safe container or loaf pan. Cover with plastic wrap, and freeze until firm, at least 3 to 4 hours.

Makes about 1 quart

Metric Conversion Chart

Unless you have finely calibrated measuring equipment, conversions between U.S. and metric measurements will be somewhat inexact. It's important to convert the measurements for all of the ingredients in a recipe to maintain the same proportions as the original.

General Formula for Metric Conversion	
Ounces to grams	multiply ounces by 28.35
Grams to ounces	multiply grams by 0.035
Pounds to grams	multiply pounds by 453.5
Pounds to kilograms	multiply pounds by 0.45
Cups to liters	multiply cups by 0.24
Fahrenheit to Celsius	subtract 32 from Fahrenheit temperature, multiply by 5, then divide by 9
Celsius to Fahrenheit	multiply Celsius temperature by 9, divide by 5, then add 32

Approximate Equivalent by Volume			
U.S.	**METRIC**	**U.S.**	**METRIC**
1 teaspoon	5 milliliters	2 cups	460 milliliters
1 tablespoon	15 milliliters	4 cups (1 quart)	0.95 liter
½ cup	120 milliliters	1.06 quarts	1 liter
1 cup	230 milliliters		

Approximate Equivalent by Weight			
U.S.	**METRIC**	**METRIC**	**U.S.**
½ ounce	14 grams	1 gram	0.035 ounce
1 ounce	28 grams	50 grams	1.75 ounces
1½ ounces	40 grams	100 grams	3.5 ounces
2½ ounces	70 grams	250 grams	8.75 ounces
4 ounces	112 grams	500 grams	1.1 pounds
8 ounces	228 grams	1 kilogram	2.2 pounds
16 ounces (1 pound)	454 grams		

LEARN TO MAKE MORE TREATS WITH STOREY BASICS

Storey BASICS®: The essential information you need to get things done. With dozens of topics to choose from, Storey BASICS are the ideal entry point for anyone wanting to acquire new skills and become more self-reliant. These portable, highly accessible guides, written by seasoned experts, provide the perfect amount of information to ensure success right from the start.

How to Make Chocolate Candies by Bill Collins
Making candy at home is fun and delicious! Turn out an array of sweet treats in no time with easy techniques for tempering chocolate, boiling sugar, filling molded chocolates, and much more.
96 pages. Paper. 978-1-61212-357-8.

How to Make Frozen Yogurt by Nicole Weston
Use standard ice cream makers to churn frozen yogurt that's smooth, tangy, and lower in fat than ice cream. The secret is in Nicole Weston's special meringue method, described in simple detail.
112 pages. Paper. ISBN 978-1-61212-377-6.

Making Vegan Frozen Treats by Nicole Weston
Make 50 creamy, vegan desserts to satisfy your ice cream cravings. Almond, coconut, and soy milks replace dairy milk and cream in these classic and contemporary ice cream flavors. Also includes fruity sorbets and granitas.
96 pages. Paper. ISBN 978-1-61212-390-5.

These and other books from Storey Publishing are available wherever quality books are sold or by calling 1-800-441-5700.
Visit us at *www.storey.com* or sign up for our newsletter at *www.storey.com/signup*.